THE HABITABLE WORLD

THE HABITABLE WORLD

Beth Anderson

Instance Press
Santa Cruz CA
2001

Grateful acknowledgement is made to the editors of the following publications, in which versions of poems in this book appeared: *Arshile, The Baffler, Bivouac, Dad, Duration, East Village Poetry Web, Five Fingers Review, The Germ, HOW2, Proliferation, Windhover,* and *An Anthology of New (American) Poets* (Talisman House).

"The Domain of Inquiry" was published as an Instress chapbook and is indebted to Marianne Moore and *The American Heritage® Dictionary of the English Language.*

"In Residence"was published as a chapbook by Pressed Wafer.

I would like to thank Keith Waldrop, Rosmarie Waldrop, Jennifer Moxley, Steve Evans, Renee Anderson, and John Marx for invaluable contributions to the project of the author.

Cover design by Renee Anderson

Instance Press
327 Cleveland Avenue
Santa Cruz, CA 95060
www.poetrypress.com/instance

Instance Press titles are available from Small Press Distribution, Inc.:
(800) 869-7553
orders@spdbooks.org

CONTENTS

THE DOMAIN OF INQUIRY

IN RESIDENCE

The necessary idealizing of you reality
is part of the search, the journey
where two figures embrace

This house was drawn for them
it looks like a real house
perhaps they will move in today

—Barbara Guest, "An Emphasis Falls on Reality"

The habitable world forms a complete circle, itself meeting itself.

—Strabo, *Geographika*

EVIDENCE

ARRANGEMENTS

It's a small dream, that of silence   and dry, how to use
mayhap   Another desert entered the landscape
and left us with this one, asking what remains
aside from a ponderous leaf flying and *siren* the verb

Finally people moved
though they were understood as part of the architecture
or the poise this evokes, hand just so
and others appended   In choreography
wished into then out of sync
existence gathered and unraveled in a number of beats
resembling the syllabic

Relish the initiate sounds
and what whey will become as they leave a throat
Reminisce with me, for we once sprang into motion
while famished   heraldry across one rough stone
kept us going when the spurious wind declared itself
and the harvest went bad while still in the ground

This has always been a familiar passage
We couldn't claim ourselves from the lineup but did desist
en masse we did one thing we wanted
but that's another key   and the softest part of the animal
Fiction beckons from outside as if by leaving
at least rerouting   punctuation would give pleasure
From pews in which one sat and lost

another followed and thus association bore

the seconds we called out   wished again for another alphabet

larger than the boy on the stoop

and an alumnus darting across the screen

who apprised us that false dawn is out of books, is dried

to hang from a beam and hung mindlessly in

a pattern unlike its rhyme   Our plan became irrelevant

like music discharged from a window or the gesture made

in response   hoping to subsist on idolatry and larkspur

a series so smooth made the leap easy to take

Occasional Movement

Light assembles then removes itself
in veneration, mannered, care
so taken redundant in name:
be thine forever is a conundrum
underlying attempts to structure boundary

As if ripened in one paper bag
we glow gradually, surface
from urges to take and donate
into a reconstruction of what seems
to have occurred: an opportunity
arising   Pained steps
encircled shadows and persons
yet made space for others

the bright glare of instructions
flung against the time of day and
the daunted, driven from one site
to the original abode
as if part of a sequence torn from
and reattached to narrative

I am longing for structure
for your recounting to illuminate mine
Attempts at description linger
alongside heaps of snow
and rules clouded by

directionless cries recalled
Some lines cut across, depict
while others provide a surface
for circuitous behavior

procedure so involved
that the observation of beauty
cannot take place   Casual hills,
some casual climbing of them,
articulate what might be detected
in the dense undergrowth
padding broken gates
and the language
that accompanies their breaking

A visit was made   We must have arrived
or received, passed beverages from
a makeshift sideboard to
expectant hands, allowed
the fitting of conversation
into places held for dark query

This reply owes its existence to a room
paneled in glass and flowers, to activity
repeated and framed
by luminous color

as if desire
or some mirrored event
were encircled by hands
gesturing concern and the cavalier

in a balance which births *exit*
in the brief interlude
between intent and attainment
Their steady flashes freeze
into clues, carefully drawn
pools singling tap from tap
or metals correlating to sheens
encompassing other substance

LINGUALITY

The genus term is silent, a chance that disdains
all imagery despite its own portrait, passive and coiled.
There is discretion in a love for the bilingual, a sensual morass
of alphabets, a finite number of syllables to attract you

to a past and its promise. The same products are available
and road signs remind us of home, to undertake
archetypes knowingly, to put in a bus line, a curb, a tile-lined
clawfoot tub. More gravel in the face is an improvement

like the wooden ball clutched by an eagle's talon
and the self-correction implicit in keeping the chest open.
A monogram is part of this property, part of mellifluous speech.
Can we simply not record the streamlined journeys?

The financial report you could understand but not explain
is beneath the novel in my case. The placement is indicative.
The book's jacket is rough-edged and dark. I understand the appeal
of the floorcloth or a stone wall, herbs gone wild alongside

a flagstone path that leads past the house and toward fruit trees,
a site where we thought creatively. Assessing what is important
happens to be part of the job, the first language approached
from within the second. What it thereby takes on and from me.

FLOAT AND LAND

Excuses repeated thrice daily cease to be identified as such
become philosophy that may float in time, take on traits of a doctrine
followed simply for how it is written down   Hand and font

help themselves beneath a row of figures admitting nothing
despite similes ready to encompass the smoke
absented when heads complete the motion of turning, a way
in which to enter a room with hooks and no curtains

Light opens to words provided by the atmosphere, strung by conversation
in an unfettered space that could have walls   could eat everything
if made into meals   Plains beneath begin to prepare
for something to land as we speak from across the street

reminding that silences fill themselves with whatever is available
The smog blended with each sound   twisted
posture made when weight borne is not balanced across the back

EVIDENCE

The hollows   the metal details made to support and confine
Like fog covering parts of buildings some chronicles
can be foreseen while others are surprises, an assembly of scents
camouflaging one another   Abrupt   the grey air
the seams which show the making of some object rendered vague

Each time we cross a river I try to name it
but cannot envision a map of these routes, crisscrossing
what should be a scripted life   No longer simply that
which is pulled from a drawer prior to travel
instituting *memory* as a byword, instead

my figure   imagined   is the equivalent of a wet clothesline
to the left, of an abandoned smokestack further up
the glimpsed conglomerate   Some tissue ripples as a form of notation
and sawdust floats off   Then, we roamed the city
on determined feet, unveiled skills seldom applied

No motion suffices   Nothing edible appeals   In small cavities
scattered along the coast, swathed with what storms carry in
the script transfigures pressure into tongues
shapes of sentences in illuminated sand
inspired by wind and fauna and shocked into form by voice

Who can tell what holds together layers of wood
or who painted one ragged metal sheet with the word *end*?
Around the house are drums to hold oil and the planning of
what has been identified as a reasonable day   This lushness
suits its own setting, including time

away from which you have temporarily stepped   as a terrified animal
scuttles against the house's edge, disrupting
those rich wheels called love   If only the spokes
were of metal or the space beneath the stairway empty
then our stitches could be removed   a surreality in the proper room

No flat spaces   Some parallel lines   These are named for
anticipation, for a level of the personal flickering
as clouds trail off   a neighborhood's borders undone by murky air

In Readiness

A geography for your character can be learned
only after the blind cord frays. I feel impatience,
a gift perhaps, but when applied in retrospect
only a small comfort brought hence
across a footbridge, over carelessly spaced boards.
As if expecting a lamp to be lit by someone else, I await guests.
Await inexactitude. Whether or not you comply
I'll glide across the lawn in my head, away from roses planted
before we moved here or moved together at all. Herein
my reward, with grace we can settle into
as water streams down the panes and our breath condenses opposite.
In search for transport, a new cut spurns its source,
and absolution is all we need now to become complementary.
The vicinity calls out bookishness and chastises those
who have put off visiting for so long, but I like it anyway
and once again look past the rings on the table, treated
like a wing. Treats the medium like air. A deterrent unfurls
above the buildings in view, so gentle like its own breeze
so creatively laid out like all we choose among,
stark in labor, light before. Unable to generate
anything but noise we settled for thought, sorted out
whose errors were whose and added these to accumulations.
The time laid aside for further mulling has healed
into rope and twisted on itself while we idled nearby
in a game. Now that we have learned all this
an application can be sought, undone, a glistening lake.

DESPITE HEAT THREATENING

Imported as effort
a style of instruction which
acknowledges gold petals among communiqués
strewn over the floor   hanging from curtain rods
still bodies refresh by remaining still

and gesturing at capacity
has become the only method
a horizon that curves
not the flat line seen up close to be a future
thick layers of the previous century within a text

for which there is no cure
in daily and details   Plan an ideal over again
an imagined world not in order
to create landscape but to be weighed
against perspective   skilled presentation is

a ruddy substitute for reticence or sheets
a straining to possess   Under the stairs
having handled grief as if it were some other word
contortions have trailed
a series collected here   resisting capture

and patterns in cloth   always with the same plates
as acrobatic syllables brought together form delays
counteract a coaxing shape
What is suspected to be external
beneath a well-lit ceiling

 are accusations hurtling sight toward public identities
and inclusions of bias wrap
flavor   whether flattened by natural disaster
or removed on a whim   reflections
will determine how the house is seen

In the dim window what is shirt and
what is skin cannot be told
around faint static   a look of vast purple field
seems satin-lined so that you rush past it   count all figures
as drama pounds the frame

WESTERING

The conditions were not adverse, the impulse
not absent. Able to look away from livery
we caught a reference that would change our lives
and bliss followed along with other conditions,
including one half-empty glass just in time
to haunt. Only then did we relate our story
for history spurs on all progress. Feeling regional,
we represented city blocks with napkins
and passed entrance after entrance
en route to the riverbed. New patterns, old plans,
these should be priorities but then holding the door
gets in the way or the wine list arrives.
Assured of a new pair if these wear unevenly,
I feel ready to face objectivity. But
the trick of relaxation has yet to be understood.
Though named, it is part of a cabinet
waiting to be finished. With one answer
we learned how insipid the auditorium had become
so left and saw keys moving by means
of a mechanism concealed in the pavement
like a star or a path leading up the hillside
as a result of floodwater. One letter looks in this light
like two separate symbols, as if nicknaming our century.
It took one full week to choose postcards
and we were distracted by addresses

for higher altitudes suffer too,

and it is hard to keep track of what is desirable

with this damp and transient map.

ALLEGED ORIGINAL

Absence inspired a wish to be unknown
as the occasion shifted with a suspect preference
for moving away from the current into the imagined
luxurious sea, a little bow to the recycling plant.

By some weather? Beyond this one there's a life
and pink sand empty of sharp objects and dead things, demonstrating
variety of species with some sort of metaphor

moments of questioning whether a story will emerge
or leave the pristine for some other assignation. This memory of *garden*
pretends to be nothing else, nothing but an idea
made solid through transplant. Venues grown elsewhere
help form a long bridge crowded with cars all intent on one another
and devotion, move slowly through it until we are prepared

in the awkward stillness. Portraiture in bright sun
is blissful until it meets a central construction of pond and footpath,
water in the form of making air visible. That which we think
occurs only to the graceful is manifested beyond. Purposes elude. Silences

do not. The daring of the shorn, two of the same creature
split by cultivated plants can provide no evidence
in body or other, earlier imitation. Though *disembodied* may feel like
a familiar passage it must be observed that singing does echo
both from one mythology of a large rumbling storm and from
a morning opening into a crowded room. So quiet I could hear my ears ring.

But here among collisions there is not enough preparation
for summer violence, water waiting to spread the streets
and dry trunks swirling into a forest around us. Beneath the changing sky

considering whether happiness is reminiscent of a heavy axe
waiting for use behind a sheet of glass, there are ways
in which a town may be killed off. If we wanted to snake along
this would be doing it. Rows of buttons and ties, of backyards merging.

Around the mobile scenery a system of activity could be
a precedent overturning itself or could be a box containing emergency tools
suddenly unsealed, leaving us idle among feverish abandoned rakes
and clippers. What nonsense is amid the senses? Some impersonal
coat of arms was once a marshland, now is a refusal not only to read

but to clean anything made of wood or conduct electricity, exuberant enough
to distract the inadvertent phone call from the size of the room
its open windows and the long flat morning visible through them.

Natural Law

A Balanced Selection

It is the nature of things to believe
in some *if-then* in situ adjoining faith
and philosoph. A solution terrifies the surface
on which writing rests, as though
melting would not condemn the twig
to reference, to object taken up and assessed.
And as questioning is added to my list
of questions the room spins to a halt, the surface
brings up childhood, the song helps us launch
collective enterprise. Working
to establish rational discourse rather than
a supreme model was behind all effort.
We forgave ourselves for our livelihood
when the table turned into a campfire and our tales
grew fantastic, tearing up comic books to feed it
and listening without learning a single lyric.
Flattery may get you somewhere after all.
It appears to proceed according to the odds
of winning the lottery in one state,
to etched-out patterns in another, wavy lines
on a topographical map echoing breath.
Yet my query about daylight-saving time
goes unremarked day in and out, perhaps due
to a memory of highway noise
heard from a house above its flow.
If the hills do change color in place of leaves

then departure will be easier than not showing up
to begin with. Ignoring the problem of intrinsic sense
leads to lewd description of real life,
entwined with a refusal to titillate. Broken into sublaws
that allow a cathedral to be built, the workings
of humanity at first appear coincidental, then hike up
in price past dealership. The break between evolution
and standing reverent may be what has made us human,
 some music-like phrase underlying limb from limb
a grasping beauty. It gives a greeting unchanged
by societal position, in a voice that cracks
according to what is inherited rather
than environment. Paradise has reopened its portals
just in time to avoid sin, but will close on the rational mind.

FOR POSTERITY

With a straight face the claim was made that language exists
in order that Earth may be regarded as garden rather than war zone.
How is another story altogether. And thus the teller transmogrified

into tale. When it was all recorded and sealed in a lavender envelope
we argued about the percentage of pink the color contained.
Beige and *rose* were tossed about like weaponry, caught by their handles

and swamped in death. Numerous such truisms thrived in our community,
drawing folks from one another into studies of layout. Where this tent
resembles a tent seen on film, the majority are cabins

constructed of paper-trimmed logs. *Acting is the thing,* quoted one counselor,
so imagine being a campfire. Pretend to write letters home complaining
about the quality of minutia, black fly, canned goods, the general lack

of imagination submerged beneath burning newspaper. Now that revisions
have become background and my voice has cleared itself
of misanthropy, our tableau can accept the trappings of peak season

which is projected to fall next week and may be foreshadowed here.
Perchance we shall become the pronunciation that brings familiar comfort
in from the memorable cold, protecting this set of accordion doors

that keeps noise out. Any chance of chill will be labeled with masking tape
while we sleep. Coping with dual bewilderment of recordkeeping and
contentment has installed a mobile above the table, haunting the room

with error-laden attempts at exchange. We managed to translate one-third
of the document, and while I would not ridicule our labors, neither
would I live among them willingly. This turned into full-scale rejection

 somewhere along the verbal causeway, a strange character scratched
in clear glass where paint has been rubbed away. Where the chips landed
a way was sketched out, captured without category or a wide-angle lens.

A Record Overheard

Merely heard at heart, in seasonal bliss
the view from the tower has become history.
The cart before the horse, some say, and
out of the confessional booth all talk sounds lurid.
But since that symbol
there have been any number of tomes read
by eyes meeting, by meeting in corridors,
on rooftops, with purpose.
Enter the blackbird. Enter great gems
revealed when rough stone is broken. The need
for a chisel can be consuming
when marble resembles a cut of beef despite
chicken and egg jokes. My refusal sits in a bin.
The brown paper wrapped around bay leaves
takes on their dust, the dust being part and parcel of giving.
Sometimes the very moment is made by luck,
or at least notices its own fortune
in time for the telling. He that causeth rugged landscape
must alternate with time then caution future longings
against architecture and tapestry.
What these try to do with vision
has to do with sense, reconquest and congregate
sounding off. All the library had to do
was withstand flooding
and even this was too much. A center for street life
came from popularity and climate control,

not unlike some mountain stronghold

preparing for siege with every available body.

But what is regained will then be changed

by the act of its acquisition, whosoever may coincide.

A STATELY ENTRANCE

A store of natural riches formed steps
that would echo in equally rich halls.
We had dreamed of science, for from the stance
of the uneducated it was easy to do so.
Because I understand nothing of reason
I am able to support its pedestal. That is a quote
from my own records. Dreaming is another.

Three factors destined to exist in turn
became a series of demolitions. Yet unlike prehistory
this time renders fossils left and right
and preserves them in full view of censure.
The largest crane has become a subject
for prolific dabblers and then of rabid prose.
What a system here founders with noteworthy strains

that climb walls and screen doors and lend credence
to legend or at least preconception. Avid to assimilate
but avoid being seen, we correspond with the select few
and wipe the table down. That again is a quote from
somebody's dream, somebody who queries. *One*
was the native vigor until suspended for impropriety

then another pronoun chimed in to take the fall.

Welding followers, fitting assurance into an inner state,

these acts give credence to the vitality we have heard

some circles generate. The scope held by tradition

from the sidelines can prove that mastery

lacks the weight of something held in common.

CAUSALITY WITH DOCTRINE

Causality may be first cause
or scientific research. Among
men like yourselves
an inborn creativity generates
the lulling turning of pages, a
seamless carousel kicking cans
down ratted streets in time with recollection
as you will recall. *Vibrant life is for the taking*
was one claim, but another struck a real chord
and we went with it. The modern idea
of the infinite has become an era unto itself,
even another century altogether
if measurements underfoot are wanted.
Deranging vocals into wishes
is ninety-nine percent of possession
but I still lack correspondence.
Internalizing the tarot was a mistake
and a motif in sober accents
could not stop me despite my understanding
of truth, but you could have done it
if you had been in time to see
the unexpected miracles for yourself.
When holidays became facile
we turned to elementary phenomena
as if the laws of origin could be launched,
yet another thing I might do. Nonetheless

the actual is a gathering of hearsay

written downtown, meanwhile,

in ever-lessening light.

A Tally Kept

We must render ornate technologies without babble
and into a tower, visually concrete. Typically
we must render ornate the differences between counting
the number of broadly mathematical streams and
thinking about symbols. What rays will be identified
as empathic. Striving with all material on hand,
two currents met as if they shared a stream, as if
building a dam was as easy as to teach as the two-step.
In algebraic terms, our world became a place
to say *Yet* and *It was* in response to questions
about free speech and other nonconformities
or to deny eighty years of collected moss. A new culture
seems to emerge from ruined land. This law of motion
deals with what can be stopped and what causes static.
So woolen measurements are taken with the eye
not ingenuity, not lengths of steel etched with blueprints
for statues. Gridironed monuments. *Gargantuan* is
a word we avoid in general use and pull out for
moments such as this, demonstrative displays
of just how much we need that sprawling parabolic mirror.
How much the mirror needs us is parallel to page and word.
The creative role we play in evolution is based on
an obsession with the eye and whether it can encompass
the days before steamers did their duty to the lowlands.
The duty done by land imagines country
that did not resemble countryside, trying to explicate

particular varieties and technique that demands to be
rehearsed into second nature. Happenstance bought a ticket
to see this story, its deep-rooted interest in masonry.
These rings came from the gutter. I cannot disbelieve
any voice that repeats to me the tale, an honesty
saving honest mistakes in wedlock.

Learning Finds a Place

Thrice nine made an impact on education for which the world
was unprepared. A famous man living in the neighborhood could
be he who calls himself a place, could be disguising his sex

with humanistic doctrine. All in all, the light dims perpetually
but cannot be otherwise molded. The house gives me a sigh
when I ask it to, especially moving when occupants lend

their versions of drains, of winding grape vines, of the system
making up nature on a daily basis. Our own may be distinguished
or may be drowned in the three principles that were lost

immediately upon the date of their recording. As I read this,
you will wonder whose voice is heard. It cannot be that
of the person I see. A sense newly added to the list makes seven.

Our favorite medium, the fruitful guess, provides the whole burden
with an historical basis for aggression that has traditionally rested
with the aggressor. But that is only according to record, whose

singular grasp may as well be of water, learning to clutch dynamics.
The autonomy of the natural world struggles with its own demons
which again makes my voice into a question. To query the speaker

replaces a closed cosmos with evolution, industrial cogs, and
the dry riverbeds that must have preceded the wheel. I would
but rattle among sanded pebbles, trying out vision rather than dream.

Where Arches Rest

If our purpose was to follow the path of the sun
like one space left between two of the same word
then what is the *if* we leave for poetry? An elliptical space
that is really all one line, every third word skipped over
like a child's game, writing itself into a state of bliss
that comes into being when adrenaline disappears
into character. Like scenery awaiting attention, shining
coins underwater round out diatribe and make form new.
Telling tales out of school means only that the room
has a history told and untold in time with time.
One reason. Always one point of admiration, one word
on a line. There may be no space for it here
but make this into fifteen if you please
or multiply it into formula. This series may be named
for something named for another, and it may reflect
my tumultuous loneliness as well as the change of season.
Something less tony, weighted down. Maidenly attempts
have no place here with the haunted tone and love of it,
loving the literature that results with unjust due and
abandonment. The opposite of thinking too little
may turn out to be a means of disconnection, or
taking on naturalistic fervor before it is spent. When
we arrive at a mountainous foot, with quarry fleet
and meaning its own lithe nature and nothing more,
profits will empty from our minds. The horizon
will best the backyard at last. If it is truly within

the scope of the divine, as we look up at the hip roof

that has outlasted mortality, then our mysterious spring

will be explained. Death will not, but the house built

as a green frame we fit into must suffice, just as this plant

that is not holly still resembles it. Whether that question

is a reason to mislabel stands aside in the face of good reading.

The problem may be solved by a move and stroke of luck.

PAGES

A month runs down the list but checks off nothing.
No item is a good item, and if colloquialisms fall from my tongue
its fluency will remain unquestioned, itself a near-thing.

What is triumphant? What form to formulate, the bed or the sheet?
Choose *on* and move on, somewhere some advice
reaches a conversation. That accolade was misplaced, as most are,

and ancestry now reaches for a serious tone. As I learned
about my predecessors, concurrently did I decide to denounce them.
In 1841 would I have been looking at a podium?

The question of country relates to that of the type of wood used to build.
This tiny town makes my mind race. It is a place inviting immigration,
from bare ideas to steamboat tickets. Leaving for the ranch or at least the vineyard

means leaving so that a place can become a romance generations on.
My role is to access that storybook and dream about it. Attribution
of my taste to the hillside would be simplistic and is thus difficult to crush.

What is triumph? Difficult to cease what wishes to be quenched.
The records kept by verbacious borders entwine with water running
under the house, toward county land. If I don't stop now

I'll start recounting your photograph and diploma, gambling
on the horizon's history of encouraging risk
in the wanton manner of the younger generation.

Here I recognize my own laborious placement. Here the formica
is stained in a legible smear. Next the poem should be written back to fore
but that too claims witness, which breaks down too often when relied on.

The expulsion from paradise has acted with authority and saved me.
The nick of time is not too far off-base even if it is but a crude example
of earthly belief, confined to a small plot behind the days

of three known continents. A ticker marks off the manner in which the fourth
made itself evident, sliding under land as if it were snow enclosing habit,
detailed and fairly accurate but destined to fade into the ordinary.

THE DOMAIN OF INQUIRY

Query:

To live according to the lunar calendar may
depend on the reach of evident new growth,
available from want ads. The first decisive article
refers to the clergy, planning an exit
to escape announcement. Whether the proper form
accorded to subversives is a hulking presence or blends
with woodwork was not a question until the postwar era.
Our walls have the noise factor of a hallway and
a glorious arrogance. Your refusal to speak
will be written into the ridiculous with one call. Until then
a movie is in the making, and awaiting an offer helped us
survive dying plants, postmarks, and a restricted view.

Comment:

Dependent on rainfall the bows we take will restrict
views of the players. The sartorial effect
is to set the stage with a lineage ready for enunciation
or a near-saint being canonized. My answer is in two parts,
one, that atmosphere must not distract and, two, that
we need the hills of Tuscany to represent legend.
In most cases it is enough to say *to really help*
and omit *if you want.* The long table is set
with artichokes and corroded silverware
surrounded by bowls of dipping sauce. Passed around
the table some pass out, others unleash a complaint
or sign on. They kept the lead and that is warranted.

Query:

We need the hills of Tuscany to reorganize themselves
if that is warranted. Where visitors wait
so also a strain of ballads may dogmatize faith
that output will double in one year's time. It works
but defies explanation and is therefore not unusual.
Despite spurious adjustment similar in volume
to any other torrent, our plans waited in large caves
instead of lumbering into the road with the other vehicles
and thus remained intact, if irrational, sounding
in their stress like repairs being made on the world ripped in half.
Clearly my natural impulse is to choose one hemisphere
or the other, but I've been taught to sew and so set to it.

Comment:

And thus remaining intact, a new age will become
set in its ways. Today I signed off on a detail
whose phrasing may turn into culpability or the dark
green shade of a banker's lamp. Whether they decide
to live together or not, a cliché is in the making
and all the onlookers know it. Stalling is a shabby
way out and can lack a certain helpful formality. You
must also never stomp aboveboard and avoid
sustenance of a fractured skull, although playing
the market may be an alternative route. The alarm bells
cough like creditors or dependents, according
to the side of the road from which they are audible.

Query:

Must we stomp the floorboards into submission like
audible memories of friendly fire? *Thus* and *thusly*
attempt to lock and pin our talk of causality, and
ownership is one more hurdle looking to be toppled
but at least I return books when I am through.
Unsigned contract or not, I cannot ignore the call to redistrict.
Though in speech affection comes under the heading of affect,
we should try to move with the times before giving in
to that dated calling. When I first noticed my own
feelings of adventure I formed a V with my arms
until the subway air came to seem almost floral and the stoop
teemed with writers, counting airplanes passing overhead.

Comment:

Until the subway aired its grievance, patriotism was found
on every platform, a burgeoning mechanical democracy
circling like stones at the base of a waterfall. A stroll
takes us past innumerable practicing pianists and brings home
the density of air in this town center like nothing has before.
The convenience of outside forces cannot be overestimated
and when the imperative enters the scene, all cues will gasp
in relief. If the light were to advise us as to what is permissible
and what is underground, I think it would say to omit *this is*
from the conundrum. Any long-standing prescription is ripe
for fencing, and after considering penalty kicks
I pleaded to be swept along but spoke in imagination alone.

Query:

To live according to a calendar has become the backbone
of imagination, a first month ending and becoming the last.
Wearing the garb of latter and former, a new noise hunts
for a form. I came to understand the headings, learned
not to call them forth after doing work with what *no* evinces.
A preference for *kin* or *kind* became a matter of structure,
not failure, but wiser men than he have been outwitted
by systems of speech. It is sometimes contended that type
cannot satisfy and that governing unpermissible sounds is a task
to be delegated until it disappears. In contrast, every year
births a new engine. In the middle of mediation he was distracted
by plastic as a compound — partially recycled, a renewable
resource — and the fly buzzing between it and the screen.

Comment:

Bylaws of systematic speech cannot make stamina less urgent.
Screening applicants and pedal pushing add to
the number of extra steps climbed and the consequential
improvement in the view. As when we learned about popery
and the servants who keep things abstract, my coveting
extends to outlook. Makeshift linens hanging ragged
like knuckleballs somehow suffice and even succeed.
The illegalities were both bright and hideous, weeds blooming
to vie with hothouse growth for the title of most improved.
Then light transpires, emerges from secrecy to count
on target dates like the abacus formed by a fat hand's fingers
and reverses horsepower to coincide with coaxing.

Query:

Improvement in the view left us breathless, but internal
coincidence with adjectives still goes on. A fervid shuffling
leads to the only accessible vista, and where
that will leave us when the searing heat designates
place as place is as yet undetermined. But for now my artifacts
refrain from triggering any kind of strike, and we are able
to allow ourselves to like the city by rejecting its interior.
An ardor for fun was damped by dying houseplants only
when we climbed down, and in fact this timely transition
inspired yet another point of departure. We tried
to counter dismal tales of sodden counties, and success
promised to be ours but like lady luck reneged.

Comment:

Besieged with promises to be faithful, we forgave our landlord
though with misgiving. Nothing could stop us from removing
our shoes until we heard the mowers all around, for
I don't mind clutter until it collects past the first hedge.
Nursing all kinds of wounds, from papercuts to swipes
with a breadknife, rebellion curls up under the radiator,
for being the source is as large a responsibility as being the recipient.
Some gardeners relax in season, but the troublesome youth of mint
can incite dates of proposed achievement to declare themselves
in writing all over the walls. My trek to filled land allows me
some wandering but does not necessitate it, encompasses
displaced sidewalks and the normalcy of trees overhead.

Query:

Written on the walls are initials, reminiscent of carving in
trees overhead, as if the wallpaper were from a scroll that had been
carried around the world. A truculent dictator would seem to me
to require an adjective more forceful than *troublesome,*
but admitting incertitude saves your answer from placidity.
The following involve recent coinages or extensions
of primary senses: bellicose, the inspiring of fear,
the gesture that inspires description. Whatever led me
to revive my feast day was looking out for my best interest
and the act of feasting became its own
translucent object, artistic as the slope of a branch joining
the neck without interruption before the wind bows down.

Comment:

The world is too precise to be a document, pieced to withstand
the wind, selvage to selvage. I imagine a certain demeanor
and then it appears, manifest in the long window over
the front porch. A voluntary stain coaxes you hither and makes
a case in turn for keeping to oneself when photos would encroach.
Tending the herd is one duty I will happily pass along
to a successor or even the overzealous competition. Where
is my drive? Salivating over extended evenings, budding
honeysuckle, a smooth commute. The fact is that I now can see
from my window what did form the edges of a moving train
and this changes the subject. Vantage once rocked and now
hesitates to shift. Adjustment must kick in, but until then
an unpredicted early walk expresses perfectly how time fills up.

In Residence

An Accusation Abetted

When you refuse me stories because of slight variance
I cannot clear a space for lightning. It remains veiled by environment,
prepares to sail through gorges along the river that will be
purposely flooded in twelve years, beside coal-dusted buildings
that will adorn the innards of a gargantuan lake. What we haul
across our shoulders and breathe out is drifting with the river's surface,
barely missing barges and coating the water with near-words.
It is a form of fjord, a means of holding tongue against teeth
in preparation for speech. I have never seen anything
like this balance of shore and current and so will myself to have
visual recall, using this profile as if it were the beginning of a familiar movie
to generate cues, nearly serial, nearly three thousand miles long.

The accusatory posture was accentuated with brows, arching
to voice a desire for the skeletal. Ready to admonish, fingers cocked,
we wrote *barter systems* in the minutes but did not follow up.
In each lyric was lyricism rendered by a sullen face,
by fatigue without armor, unable to tell the tale
and excuse crying wolf. Tomorrow we may strive for
the correct balance of pause and gesture, settle for learning how
to read the months as signals. Perhaps with a wave toward function
or with spread fingers hovering over floorboards, or by assigning the unruly
monosyllabic names. And then to learn that your house is not
your house but a group of stances taken together to indicate tenancy.

YONDER DRY DRY GRASSES

Yonder the meadows indicate signatures pressed into beach sand
somehow heaped between a twisted oak and soil spilled with the tides.
Tantalizing wind. We expected this momentum to be seamless
and all our preparations were as if we could rely on two remaining episodes
and details of their scripts. Changing the paper for the next day
ensures pretense will continue gently
but leveling the page and land requires a responsive interlace.
The envisioned means of coming true will either conjugate or fall.
We set that territory apart as if we meant it, leapt from bell towers when necessary
and craved happiness between times. I knew many of the streets and landmarks,
was prepared to climb and admire and enter into history
and its keeping, all for the sake, needing memory,
dallying over when to move on in the most comforted way possible.

The spaces skipped, the back would break, these can be fought
like the laboratory's resemblance to heaven. The town cudgels
its place with the locals like salt. Quality and its issues
begin to curl when neglected, tendril-headed, a clear and graphic rule
that will provide per samplers and other offerings.
Weaving through crops in order to identify botanical names
we came to the dank pool where we hoped to see portraits but settled
for dislike. Rehearsals transmuted into performance, bodies arched
to fit over bicycle racks and shoes came untied. These
were the only things about us that adjusted to the new century.
As if giving could lend credence we gave and gave
while the water's metallic taste affected vision and indicated a figure
silhouetted imprecisely where the pond had been drained.

THE ORIGINAL MOMENTUM

Give me the archetype so I can run with it, for in fatigue
the transitive means more, nodding off against the side of the car
and lolling about in time with progress. I became a character
ready to note my own response and assess it alongside
what a word means according to impulse. A mere autobiography
came to life as chatter swam. Already setting up tomorrow,
grinding coffee, knowing something will ease as the dead return to print.

Bothered by mad music, perhaps the style of the date, perhaps
we can up the ante to airports. In his or her head
something should have been learned by flipping through endless photos
of the crumpled car or at least from hearing it, but consonants
were not doubled in time, the ransom has gone unpaid.
In the plural. What counted was temperature and
requests for blankets unfulfilled, piling up. In absentia the anniversary.
By finding a quiet nook we played into the hands of our searchers
who expected we would run from bagpipe noises and humidity
before we realized it ourselves. And into a room of contention.

Claims of last words and lights flashing took up opportunity
and examples for next year's project dwindled. Did he write
of pulses and scopes, pill schedules? They exhaust, lend themselves
to wine drinking, times and places in which to forget
the looming smallest continent. The fear of persona creeps upstairs,
visits from across the ocean. Because it is foreign
it is a foreign body, taking a series of preparatory shots too late
and resting between them on the pull-out couch. The last time we moved
it was not ourselves. The first time we moved it was once.

PREPARE THE OPEN PLAINS

The tundra stretches out like people who have not met
or like stone and monument prior to construction. A perfect substitute
for the real angle. If we were willing to postpone our respite
we could triumph over mere respectability and discover a true mission.
Rather than settling for the original plan we could find shells to use
as placecards and acknowledge that a game for two is either a no-brainer
or not a game. The era of wood-based entertainment has returned
with a vengeance to extend the duration of fanfare beyond what
can be endured. Or so the rangers have claimed in my hearing
near the edges of land-grant institutions, nigh on a strike made
under pressure. We intended, not that it means much, to extinguish
totalitarian control. Viscous fruits decorate tables for display only.

To set prints permanently in the sidewalk is one goal, as fleeting
in its way as the steam rising from a just-rinsed dish.
The temporary pass will soon be revoked or made permanent.
It will depend on whether someone on staff would be willing
to save your life. I learned about types of clouds
when I learned about partnerships, came to see
that tweaking them for snow is purely better business
and that this pallidity is determined by who does the tracking.
But such specialized knowledge has not stopped me
from overt use of contractions or from kneading relentlessly my worries
as if they were in hand. The motto escaped but the island
and crosses marking treasure remain, placidly bright.

Announcing the Procedural

Passage granted by the domicile derives from your participation,
how you lend it your presence and color its commonplaces.
By bartering what was left outside the rectory door for a new reputation
we could see the change from rain to sleet and by extension understand
all urban myth. Our light banter sounds like rain, for which I am
already nostalgic. Primly clasping the hand of a revered guest
before the loft could lean any further into the storm
guaranteed a salve to apply to our desperate heritage, flight patterns
that were learned along with secret handshakes
in library stacks before the season began. Before shifty eyes.

I believed in arboretums back then. Swarms of hungry insects
leaning into trees, gatherings of dangerous animals. If the caretaker
disagrees then we will scorn him, relaying that cause and effect
as applied to pronouns will still bring about songs and singing.
On the fourth try the key will fail no matter how dogged you are
and regardless of temperature. Desire for luxe is produced by fantastic
imaginings about neighborhoods and correlations from an external site
like a park. Sitting around the patio table in a scented spring breeze
allows the reckless construction of bookshelves and the hanging
of tapestries on frail plaster walls. Allows transformation
to write itself out of its tiny taped-up plastic bag.

The tower takes precedence always, unlike collecting flatware
and mail. I reply only on occasion, for scrawling
feels forced if done religiously. Getting stuck in a cold clime
drapes the environment with glitter, chants into a cardboard tube
directed toward the glen to attract wayside glares. Luckily
this one vowel is found in most words, and the decor we dreamed up
is forgiving. Despite the ubiquitous disclaimer we all want
to find our names in text or to at least inspire character
if not an entire, ravenous zoo. Animals will eat the neighborhood
before convening in the tall grass to decide what to do with noise.

As the Color Drains

What should command attention is process, what to do
with this chronic cough. Although vainer moments exist in your history,
they are not internal and therefore pale in frustration
and physicality. Whether a misstep is an error
is open to question. Finishing the finances, figuring the weeks
and associations that self-generate, I prepare to hold my wrist thusly.
To read some samples from those letters before returning the book.

We forgot to water one plant but it lived. Our tomato vines fruit red and golden
and so eradicate concern for posture, impulses to practice sitting
or consideration of pewter helmets en route to stiff interviews,
all part of counting. The assessment of our city matters
as does my position at its foot and the number of seats occupied
without changing that relationship. Luckily the floors are thick.

A birthstone in an aluminum setting is what I coveted and saved for
like fluency, like sugar, like the perfect finger wave growing at the back
of my head. This city of birth crumbles. Its idiom is just off.
There are many statements I would prefer not to hear, citizenry, cognate,
awaiting more music and considering how to work with light behind me
and a madrone tree in front, waiting to be put into the text.
Preferential treatment becomes prose. Speech down the street
rearranged its own garble into a claim that we grandly ignore,
misspelled and all, not thrown by the shape of the sky.

HAIL

As we watched, something nameless conquered the section. Like all
sounds heard through the conduit of wall infrastructure
wearing an old outfit to a new party matters. Gradually wears down
what we have worked for and can cause permanent damage.
As likely however is permanent risk, buckling some office beams
until they resemble pumpkins more than rooms, more than coaches.
It is part of an arena not presented in the workplace before,
constructing in the dark, staggering down implements.
Expectancy lowers like a reflex when faced with reunion.
So you claim, but I sense your adrenaline as surely as I feel irritated
by the cheap yellowing pages of my mass-market paperback.

Mending buttonholes, sewing on buttons that closely resemble
the originals, these are tasks meant to soothe before the big night
starts to chew and tries to spit. A bond with specificity
was carefully maintained, meted out weekend by weekend
by claims of friendship. Before finale became pomp
I tried to chat easily as if tea sat before me, ready for sips
between witty disclosures. We all desire the delight of recognition
and even admit this, but it is not easy to see through these
prerecorded sounds. It could be out and about, looking at scenery
and wishing for experience. There is surely much more to wish for
but in attending to the seated and ignoring the passersby
what *pedestrian* really means oscillates between nothing and more.

A Deed of Title

When I came to understand myself as able, I sent word to the island
and nearly made it around before ownership changed and
distracted me into misinterpretation. Always abrupt, such transference,
but we will meet again where names are shortened and the familiar
is like a housepet swimming in its cage. Where the air thins
earth takes another name, announces its frugality
despite a supply of views that will never dwindle. We leadenly swam
to an escalation and traced our shape in its paper wingspan.
Numbers of pebbles made up a stark beach below us, one by one
nearing the surf nigh upon a fortnight and an imminent bestseller.

This is the best reversal I have witnessed in recent memory
like skin split across the knuckles due to neglect rather than malice
or spring cleaning in another season. When an act is traditional
then who can argue with it? A little luck must fall whether or not
it mirrors the mood, not mired in the day-to-day or in response
to a legal claim but fraught with reflections. We lean on the power
of envelopment, of pretense, of weaving among streetlights
ready to listen or sing. The loneliest night is still in dispute.

We reviewed but could not categorize the explorers, diplomats,
leaders of revolutions, and spouses. In some cases
tweaking made a slot. In others we simply signed off
and left the floaters in fluid. A sphere of land recalls the slope
of a chapel into a confessional booth and how sound catches my ear

as I release my hands. From his cupola one inventor generates
a pattern for traverse based on stellar observation, enhanced
with twinges in underused limbs. Another reason to take the stairs
is based on the sway of this building as we pass by
and how it interacts with discomfort before circumference
makes the circular out of a referent and into itself.

Any Proper Escapism

Treading the outdoors today combined escape with obligation. Strange when
the best is also the best option, perhaps physique complicit with therapy
will drive us there. Going stir crazy is often imprisoned in connotation
despite remembering only now how that headache felt, how fingers
returning to room temperature announce themselves. Until then the belief
in warmth is itself truth. These are the function words of characters, who
can bundle up until neoromantic formulaic otherness comes to grovel,
shunned, shunned, and closed into a fraught circumstance.

These echoes of fatigue come so very close to familiarity, my companionate
sealant. Conspiracy is not undone by knowing I have seen you somewhere else,
you swinging landscape, your haunted trees. Height distinguishes. Wishing
to acknowledge addiction I place my hesitancy to the fore, near the rattle
of water in a tin basin and secure in remembered terrain. Everything beneath
the foundations of these houses is mine, the slight hillocks and the serrated ends
of faux wheat. Strangers picking berries as if the yard were a hedgerow
still find this street attractive, curving along a creek bed now cemented in place,
rumbling like the sea. We remain in a hot room as members of the intersection
move on, pass like monuments into opportunities for rebirth.

Try to find the needed interlude and do not succeed. Part of the plot
must be realized in your hands. I planned to be an heiress,
no matter the fantasy of it and the effects of connecting all forebears
to street names. Whether ceremonies accept their roles

the contretemps must learn in late autumn for themselves the genus term.
Fanciful relies on fancy and *definite* happens to be unobtrusive,
a hidden ribcage occasionally revealing itself with an intake of breath,
with each profession tested and reconfined to the bleak anthological shelves.

The Room Foretells

Whence the year, all theories of heat cannot distinguish
varietals from car alarms, both incessant in the deep night.
We are rolling toward adjectives, cruising in a convertible speedboat
that was pulled across the highway by an advocate of part-time labor.
After this there is only one more volume awaiting release,
a single lyric left to be transcribed into the foam
remaining when our city burnt down.
Sunken as if clipped into a hedge, glistening like raku
the gradual decline searches for a monitor and hopes for a bounce. Again
much action cannot be attributed although labored breathing surrounds it
and pulses clearly accelerate. We consider opting for deliverance
but cannot quest, being tied to this place, to these times
coordinated like fingernails or etched into the handles of a jumprope.

Will you miss us in the desert? If we are visible
beyond the crested buildings that reach over ridges
please note our willingness to sink and accommodate.
Cart us some supplies for our anticipated march around the cliff feet,
their rocks that will emerge as corners and become smooth walls.
We will cling to them for guidance while squinting out and down
toward once-forgotten issues of livelihood.
Must we apologize for each delay, gather and file
inexcuses for later musings in boxes specially crafted?
I had to provoke discussion somehow
and this led to mobile amendment, reliant upon marred senses
proximate to a photograph snapped to remind me that painting is another art.

Wherever *there* may become, at least we can now understand *here,*

its mercy at ending up. Clues gathered on process

tell how little we keep on hand and that every crumb

starts to be only about words. Color the rules and impact the inescapable.

Need the wherefore, despise method, release debt

with a ceremony of dim coughing in the stairwell.

Our geographical cronies lean into four corners

and watch the acclivity warily, having heard tales of a tiny studio above

and ephemerality rubbed into its banisters.

Now the Outskirts

Now back in the fringes we can tell that glaring down
ever-narrowing roads without being distracted by
their wavery environs is a skill. A pleasure. My encompassing
of coves and graves is free of resentment at last. In this way
we meander into confession. I tell you about your life
to head off the pass and you describe mine. Thus the pronouns incubate.
Thereby a small and ancient basket inspires a heist to end all others.

What is irreversible is also a side effect, a glance tripped into
an unintended pace that can take in destiny as process
rather than totem. Tantalizing trope, fluctuating future,
how you can diverge from rivulets of running water
that paint shadows of winter trees on pavement to be driven over
in a version of unrequited love. We are reproduced in glossies, built up
with smooth boards, rubbed with age like serpentine and a hand held
by another hand into its destined shape, its paler palm.

Hauling a tied bandanna's worth of change to be filed with your horoscope
we have determined our holidays for the next decade and there is no one
to intercede on behalf of fantasy. Like marks made with blue pencil
the board has exiled our cards. Like burning bridges, we don't
remember playing or which trees produce the needed sap, thin and sweet,
or wallowing in the shallows before moving downstream to fetch a raft.

When we cease to be the actors of *formulate* and *botany*

many acres will revert to habitat, freed of faith and the acts undergone

in its name. Like income, cessation must be manifested somehow

whether or not it believes the earth has a core or paper an edge.

The long sheet on which I reminisce when the sun goes down

has never before recalled so many disciplines, has not needed vision

 to justify its marginalia. Reflected in the heat-induced democracy

of space are dreams of colonies, flexible furnishings, volcanoes

and what to do in each instance should we still be of a mutual mind.

The Royal We

This new country beholds you from a tumult of routine
that will not adjust to communal living. Other people
are always looking for titles, but I wonder what to say
to avoid praise or reassurance and yet to speak. Never previously
would *conundrum* have described my language. The plush landscape
may become predatory, its redolent lust for camaraderie
counteracting the barren state covert within all green
neatly emptying into channels disguised by hardy soil and stone.

Desensitized to travel, to trowels, to the assembly of uses
to be kept in a low cupboard as long as you keep limber,
we determine to esteem even as we age. I consider you indispensable
like the faint light of evening. Sudden affinities will guard us from
nostalgia and ceremonies we encounter will not stop months
from passing and names from adapting to time. Sit together
and add on family with a generous hand, work phrases hard
while leaping onto the bandwagon, full in song. Delight is supported and
maxims abound, searching for lips of candidates. From the oracle
you moved to a stadium arrangement and I wept upon the setting
I ever pursue as if I really could live in it, wanting lushness
as imagined under snow, farmland without the reek of cow.

But I will not be a landlover who moves into the picturesque
as if it were simply a state without victims. That link wobbles
but retains its connection, the teeth of the snake cling
to its tail. When leaning into the street to avoid a train

we spot news arriving at our door so know not to go home.
The announcement was to an audience clearly biased in favor
of having a bad time then dissembling. If I never before mentioned
my lurid past, it was to save you from yourself. When you flipped over
I declined to follow. Sensing an alert reception, my reluctance searches
for an illogical replacement before crossing the above-ground tracks.
We have realized too soon a breaking of knowledge.